WHY MEN CHEAT

Are Men Genetically Predisposed to be UNFAITHFUL?

MsterH

Bloomington, IN  Milton Keynes, UK

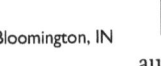

AuthorHouse™
1663 Liberty Drive, Suite 200
Bloomington, IN 47403
www.authorhouse.com
Phone: 1-800-839-8640

AuthorHouse™ UK Ltd.
500 Avebury Boulevard
Central Milton Keynes, MK9 2BE
www.authorhouse.co.uk
Phone: 08001974150

ISBN: 978-1-4343-1408-6 (sc)

Printed in the United States of America 7/11/2007
Bloomington, Indiana
This book is printed on acid-free paper.

CONTENTS

CHAPTER ONE

Cheating

A sure way to endanger your relationship or marriage is to cheat. What is cheating? Many people define "cheating" so that it excludes their own negative behavior, and meets their needs at the time. Simply put, cheating is violating the agreed upon rules, plan or boundaries (spoken or unspoken) for selfish benefit and without the consent of all parties involved. Not all expectations in relationships and marriages are verbalized, but are an inherent part of the romantic union, unless otherwise stated.

In a romantic relationship, cheating can take on many different definitions or combinations of definitions, depending on those involved and their expectations. There are no excuses for deception and dishonesty with someone you truly care about. In most cases cheating involves sex. Sexual unfaithfulness can be a "cancer" to any relationship. No definition of "cheating" has a positive connotation. Cheating is doing wrong by any standard, and in any situation.

Does "cheating" have to mean a sexual encounter with someone outside the marriage or relationship? No! If you are in a committed intimate relationship and you become intimate in any way with another person, by doing something that you know your partner or spouse would not approve of, because of how it will make them feel or react, or because it would definitely jeopardize the relationship, you have just cheated. This transgression is concealed for a reason. Usually because you realize the real implications and the probable consequences, if found out.

If you give another person outside your relationship even an intimate kiss, that you know would upset your partner, if they knew, you have just cheated. French kissing another person outside the relationship constitutes cheating. Intimate kissing is about sex, and nothing else, and is always a prelude to a sexual act. It's called foreplay! By any other name, it is still cheating. When a husband or wife comes home from work and greets their spouse with a kiss, it is usually not a tongue-down-the throat kiss, unless it's intent is to lead to a sexual encounter. It is sexually suggestive and arousing and usually accomplishes its intended purpose.

Men in general, have received a bad rap for cheating, as though women are above cheating. Well, who are the majority of men cheating with, if not with other women, who are often married or in other relationships. While it is true that more men cheat than women, just remember, it takes two!

While cheating usually turns out to have a very negative affect on a relationship and sometimes ends up being the nail in the relationship/marriage coffin, it can be an eye opener for the person being cheated on. Remember, you cannot change him. He has to want to change on his own. It is impossible, if he doesn't want to stop. He has to value you, and want to be with you badly enough to change his behavior, and prove himself worthy of your trust and your love. A word of advice: When you come to the conclusion that he is not going to change, RUN! Don't become a doormat! Cut your loses and RUN! Just because he cheated, doesn't mean that you've done anything wrong.

In a relationship or marriage, both parties should nuture and do all they can to strengthen the relationship and make it the place they want to be, more than anyplace else. Make home special and extra important to you just because he or she is there for you. Keep those flames burning so that he or she doesn't want to go elsewhere, no matter what the temptation. Remember, it's not just about him!

CHAPTER TWO

Why Men Cheat

There can be no doubt that men and women are meant to be together in love, lust and even in friendship. Both men and women have a strong desire and need to connect with each other intimately. Sex is not just a desire. It is both a need and a desire. As with food and water, the lack of sex can alter your behavior and possibly your physiological and psychological wellness.

There are those that think that men and women cannot be "just friends." It is monumentally difficult, especially if there is any physical or emotional attraction or common interests at all, between two people of the opposite gender, but is definitely possible. Totally controlling emotions is difficult, at best, but only effective until the right button is pushed.

Adultery, is one of the leading causes of divorce, or breakup of a romantic relationship, in America. Cheating, is epidemic and the finger is pointed directly at the male for his inability to remain true.

Why do men cheat? Well, there is never a good reason to cheat, but whatever the rationale, there is legitimate cause to compare men to their canine "best friends." There are lots of excuses, rationalizations and lies, why men cheat, but the bottom line is that he violated the agreed upon rules, plan or boundaries for selfish benefit, without the consent of his partner, who probably would not approve. Now he's got a secret to protect, which means, more lies.

Cheating is a violation of another person, not just the relationship and more often than not, the thrill derived, is not worth losing what you already have. At one time in America, terms like polygamy, cheating, and unfaithful, only applied to women. It was acceptable and encouraged for men to have more than one woman.

Is cheating peculiar to men? Of course not, but men are more prone to cheat than women. Some of the primary reasons men cheat are:

1. **To escape discord on the homefront.** If things are not good at home, the door could be open and you many not even realize it. Another woman will sometimes offer him just the opposite of what he's running away from and cater to his needs and and desires. If he's in a seemably unbearable and unchangeable situation at home and knows where he can find solace, he will eventually turn away, and possibly cheat.

2. **Respect and position in the house is paramount.** When a man feels that he is doing the very best he can and gets little or no respect, he will find other distractions which are more attentive to his needs and likes. The sense of belonging is extremely important to him. If he finds little proof of his reserved place with you and in the family, he will find other ways to meet his need. When he no longer pays attention to your needs, as he once did, it may be too late.

3. **Sex and intimacy are tremendously important.**
Men feel that sex is critical, though they sometimes disregard the intimacy and closeness that women so dearly crave. Sex is good for mental and physical health. Romance and sex are very necessary ingredients in good relationships. The intimacy will eventually evolve into sexual activity and is absolutely necessary for her and therefore should be a priority for him. Depriving a man of sex is creating a death sentence for your relationship. Sex is very natural and pleasurable and therefore normal for him to want it often and it is difficult for him to understand why the woman in his life doesn't want it as often. The body at some point craves the physically gratifying attention that sex provides. Always take the time to tell or show him what pleases you sexually. Let nothing get in the way of the two of you making love or having sex. Sex often decreases after the children start arriving, but why? Using the kids as an excuse not to have sex, is just that. An excuse! **Make the necessary adjustments.** Schedule time just for you and him and include intimacy. Avoiding or not making private/alone time for each other hurts the relationship. Your man will not do without

some expression of intimacy for very long. Never, never, never, use sex as a tool for "blackmail." This might work for you for a short period of time, but it almost always eventually leads to him turning his interest to someone else. He will cheat!

4. **Do not make a habit of sleeping in separate bedrooms.** Barring serious medical reasons, always sleep together, and if possible never go to bed angry at each other. Beds only have two purposes and resting is just one of them. Sometimes because of anger, resulting from an argument, one or the other will opt not to sleep in the same bed. If this happens, make it short lived. Just use it as a cooling off period and return to your joint bed as soon as possible, or this arrangement could turn out to be permanent. Be the stronger, wiser one and make up, if you want your marriage or relationship to survive, and eliminate even the thought of being with someone else.

5. **Men who lose their place of respect and honor.** Just as the woman in the relationship is the "Woman of the House," the man needs to be the "Man of the House" and all who enter this dwelling should know it. When a man

loses his position in the pecking order, which shifts between the love partners, depending on whatever boundaries have been established. It feels to him like the beginning of the end. Never place the children or anyone else ahead of him in your life. It is very common for a mother to place the man in her life on the back burner when the children start arriving. Placing him first in your life doesn't diminish the love, care or responsibility you have for your children. Just as you should be first in his life, so should he be in yours'. He must remain the"King of his Castle."

6. **Lack of Trust.** If you don't trust him and he knows it, he has nothing to lose by exhibiting less than positive behavior. Distrust breeds distrust, so likewise he will not trust you, and where does that leave the relationship? If you continue to demonstrate a lack of trust in him, he will resent it and do just what you expect that he will. A relationship without trust, respect and consideration is doomed to fail. The pressure of "distrust" is negative and destructive power source.

7. **Marriage and commitment trumps the single life-style.** A married man cannot

place the guys above time with the lady in his life. Once the single life is over, it's over. There can be no regression. Either you are married or you won't be. The behavior of single guys is contagious, because they are usually doing fun stuff, and are totally free to do so. A single man with a "significant other" is very similar to the married man, but only because he chose to be. Couples, whether married or not, should do some things together, and on a regular basis, but they both should have some "self-time," when they can do things with their friends or alone even. When he's out alone or with buddies, there should be no fear or anxiety that he'll cheat. Without space, he'll feel trapped, with a need to escape.

8. **Bad Boys or Players.** Generally speaking, women should stay away from "Bad Boys." These guys are called "Bad Boys" or Players" for a reason. They have earned this title honestly. Most are not "one woman, men" no matter what they tell you or how you feel about them. Women are drawn to them and are swept off their feet by their smooth demeanor and charm. He is usually

charismatic, attractive and very outgoing (with everyone). He's usually having fun when you see him and ignites a crowd. His behavior with women makes him a bad boy and women love being around them. They command attention. When he cheats, and he will, he's just being himself, and the women know this, and the phenomenon is that they can't resist.

9. **Abusive Men.** Men who are emotionally, verbally or physically abusive, tend to be cheaters. More often than not, they are blinded by their own perceived personal power which in reality turns out to be artificial and a weakness rather than a strength. In all cases, if a man is abusive to you, get away from him, because without an intervention, it doesn't get any better, and will probably get worse.

10. **Ex-spouses.** Ex's are called "Ex's" for a very good reason. Your man is supposed to be done with all ex-wives and ex-girlfriends. Only in the interest of common young children should he make regular visits or make a special effort to see this person. Keep

in mind that your man has had intimate sexual relations with this person, possibly for years and a some point for some time, developed a bond with this her. We all sometimes want what we can't have, and with regard to the "Ex," we know what buttons to push because we've been there and done that. Give him enough rope and he might cheat. Get involved in child visitation and personal interaction with his "Ex." It'll be uncomfortable at first, but good security is never convenient. Set the boundaries up front.

While we know that nothing is perfect and relationships aren't made in heaven, if your relationship or marriage is worth having, it is worth working for.

There is no "autopilot" button or cruise control device in relationships, at least not one that works. Like anything else worth having, your relationship requires diligence, compromise, negotiation, consideration and lots of time and hard work. It needs to be nurtured and loved. Respect is tremendously important and is right up there with our ability and desire to receive love as well as give it.

If we work as hard on our romantic relationships and marriages, as we do our jobs, hobbies and friendships, our disappointments and heartaches would be minimal. Cheating is the "Sin" of relationships and is extremely destructive to all concerned.

Women are the nucleus of relationships, just as they are the nucleus of the family unit and warrant respect. Women orchestrate the direction of a family and will do whatever it takes to make it work, but as with any "unit" she can't do it alone.

If the appropriate time and effort isn't put into a marriage or relationship, it will not survive, and cheating may not be your biggest problem.

CHAPTER THREE

Invest In Your Relationship

While it is true that no one person can change another person, we must all do our part to continually enhance our relationship and take away any artificial reasons for cheating. We must make a commitment to be happy and put in the time and effort, to be successful.

Men don't usually commit to relationships until they feel they absolutely have to. Women become solid major investors long before men and expect positive returns on their investment. Generally speaking, men want major returns with minimal investment, which is absolutely what everyone hopes for from the stock market, but a one-sided relationship will wither and die, no matter how much the one partner invests, if there's no balance.

We invest less time and energy in our relationships than we do anything else that is as important to us. Most of us make our hobbies fun and exciting and look forward to spending time playing. Our jobs demand the best of us and we find ways to perform at an extremely high level when needed. We're sometimes nicer to strangers than we are to the on we love and our life partners. We're patient and understanding with abusive customers and co-workers one the job. Our communications is never better, than with our best friends and acquaintances and we adjust daily to the needs of others.

If we invest in the stock market, we check to see how our investment is progressing everyday. **Why not the relationship?** An investment in your relationship is an investment in your life. Command and expect no less from yourself or your partner. Your relationship must be important enough to you to invest quality time, patience and energy. **It must be a priority.** Each partner must learn and attempt to meet the needs of the other as well as their own. It is imperative that each partner treat themselves as though they deserve the pleasure and respect derived from a good relationship, never "settling," for less than the value of that which they are willing to give. Just like with your "shares" of stock, you expect steady growth in their value.

If this is where you want to be and it's healthy for you, nothing should be more important. A good healthy relationship will get you through the tough times when nothing else seems to work. Nurture it and cultivate it, make adjustments where and when appropriate, and demand quality of him and command it of yourself.

Seek "balance" in all areas of your life, including your relationship, but remember, you can only control and change you and no one else. Trying to change your man is going against the grain and is like putting a raincoat on a leopard, trying to change his spots. It may work temporarily but is never a permanent fix and that behavior will always resurface, unless he makes the change.

Losing balance is not like losing sleep. You can regain and restore balance in your life through changes in your behavior and renegotiations in your relationships. We are responsible for creating our own happiness, but a lack of balance can be a definite obstacle.

Women overcompensate and make excuses for their men far too much, just to keep the peace or to make things "right." detrimental to the relationship and to themselves. Women very often make themselves responsible for his behavior and feel a need to fix him, which will always turn out to be a losing proposition. She makes excuses for him and caters to his needs and demands just to keep the relationship from failing, or so she thinks, and becomes part of the problem. Quite often women see failure in their personal relationships as a failure in life and will sacrifice all they are and all they have to keep the relationship alive, no matter how bad it becomes.

Chapter Four

Older Women, Younger Men
What's the Big Deal?
"If You Can't Find A Good Man, Raise One"

What makes it ok for an older man to be in a relationship with a younger woman, but not ok for an older woman, to be with a younger man? Middle-aged and older men are absolutely drawn to young, attractive, adult women, but usually moreso for physical reasons, than anything else.

Men are visually simulated with far more intensity than are women, though the creative imagination of a woman, is just as powerful, but less obvious. Though subtle in her approach, a woman is better at attracting men than a man is at attracting women.

There is nothing wrong with an older woman, being with a younger man, in an intimate relationship, as long as they're both consenting adults. The thought or idea of an older woman being with an attractive, substantially younger man who is exciting for her, disgusts some, but usually those who don't have a man at all, or who are unhappy with the one they have.

Society has not treated women well. Women experience lots of pressures that accompany non-traditional relationships.

Critics often disquise their envy with quick-to-judge attitudes using societal etiquette as their platform.

While age shouldn't matter in our search of happiness, society stigmatizes women and looks upon the age difference between her and her mate with extreme prejudice. Society with its multiple standards regards aging men with a touch of gray hair to be distinguished and mature looking. Women aren't so fortunate.

Women are a target for our society. Who pays serious attention to how the men at the Academy Awards presentations are dressed? Who cares where his tuxedo was made or who made it? The focus is on women and their appearance and who they're with. A woman with a substantially younger man could steal the show and become the story on page one, the following day. Women are usually their own worst critics, and that of other women.

Older women are attracted to younger men in a very sexual way and why not? Women and men no matter how old, health permitting, should be sexually intimate as long as they can and then some. Neither age nor someone else's perception of who you are or how you should live, should be a factor.

What are the odds that the younger man will cheat on the older woman? Very good. Younger women will challenge both him and the older woman. His friends are usually close to his age and like the same kind of lifestyle. The one thing that both he land the older woman have in common is sex and companionship. The older woman, with her life experiences and wisdom, is not so nieve, as not to understand this about him.

Women are very competitive. Aging women sometimes feel as though they have to make wholesale physiological changes to meet society's perception of "acceptable." Anti-aging and physical attractiveness are high their list of what's important. While there is absolutely nothing wrong with making the changes, it should be done for the right reasons. Society opinions and fads change almost daily and you can't change nearly enough to keep up. **Do it for you** and not for anyone else or to fit some other profile. You're the only one that you'll always have to live with.

Younger men are attracted to older women who have something to offer, just as with younger women who are attracted to older men. Few twenty-five year olds are on a mission to find a 60 year old man or woman, just to have fun with.

Most older women aren't necessarily on a deliberate search for a younger man. More often than not, it happens naturally as with any other "connection." **Ladies, "Just Do It."**

CHAPTER FIVE

Finances in Relationships
Taking Care of Number One First

Finance, big and small, is an issue everyone has to deal with and for most, is very high on their list of priorities, and very well should be. Dissension over finances has been the root cause for many divorces and the demise of many relationships. Much of how we live and the amount of stress we are saddled with is based on our financial situation and how we deal with it. Sudden wealth has a tendency to change behavior, for better or worse, and very abruptly. Money is power, and powerful men sometimes take on an air for invincibility. Many women are attracted to men who appear powerful and invincible. Flexing of his might often ends up in cheating.

Most men have lots of respect for women who contribute to the relationship financially as well as in other ways. For women, this levels the "playing field" and boasts their equality and entitles her to just rewards, as with him. Totally depending on him to support you will someday become a source of resentment and regret.

Money is power in any language and on any continent. The more money you have, the more potentially powerful you are viewed. If you have little or none, your life is substantially different.

All women, without exception, must have their own "financial safety net." Figuratively speaking rainy days are coming, no matter who you are, or your station in life and you'd better be ready or suffer the misery of life's uncertainties.

Far too often women who have been battered and abused find that it is tremendously more difficult to leave the home and the abuser, because they have no means of support, and no money even to take care of immediate safety and security necessities, like transportation, housing and food, etc. No matter what the plan is for leaving, it requires that you have some money. When the decision is made to leave and you have a substantial amount of money, there is much less pressure and fewer barriers to overcome, when making the move.

All people, who work for a living should keep some funds with them, for emergencies or unexpected social events. It is not always possible to stop what you're doing and run to the ATM for money and after dark is never a good time to go because of safety concerns. Working and earning money is reason enough to keep a limited amount in your purse or wallet. It symbolizes your independence, is convenient and absolutely elevates your morale and self esteem.

Men have for centuries made women feel dependent on them for financial support, an evil that has grown to bite them in the butt, through spousal support, alimony and many other means.

Never, never, never make divorce/financial decisions under duress or in anger. Many times out of anger at him, wives agree to give up the right to everything, including spousal support and household material items, just to get away from their monstrous spouse, and finalize legal divorce, especially in cases of abusive marriages. BIG MISTAKE! The chances of you getting "screwed" in a divorce settlement are pretty good, so don't make it easier by giving away your power.

A woman who doesn't work, has children to support, maintains a household and needs to have one of the family vehicles, must have some money. Being financially independent gives you lots of options and flexibility, but if you're not, you will need all the help you can get. Why not get it from the responsible party? If at a later date, you become financially independent or wealthy and want to give it back, you can always do so at that time, but it's remarkably more difficult to get it later, after having refused it in the first place. **"Take Care of Number One First."** Keeping your man, is important to you but not at the cost of "You."

CHAPTER SIX

Don't Allow Your Man to Become Worth-"Less"

Most women pride themselves in their personal appearance and go to great lengths to look good. Weight gain as we age, is natural, but this is an extremely sensitive issue with woman. Whether women do anything about it or not, they are always conscious of it.

Men as different as they are from women, are very conscious of their physical appearance though the worry factor is much lower, especially after marriage. While single and courting, he is exercising regularly, trying to eat right and spends almost as much time in front of the mirror as you do, checking his looks.

The body you were attracted to almost disappears after marriage. You can see it slipping away before our eyes.

Do not allow your man to become a slob. Beer bellies don't grow overnight. They're cultivated. Though large bellies are referred to as a woman's playground (only by married people) they are unattractive and unhealthy and costly to wardrobes.

No matter how you as his woman, perceives his new and larger body, he represents you to your friends, relatives and to the public in general, just as you are a reflection of him. In no way, allow your man to become less of a man, or less caring about his own personal appearance. If he doesn't care about himself, guess who's next.

Do not allow your man to become a "couch potato" before your eyes. He should always remain active and establish good productive reasons for getting up everyday. **Do not get involved with a man who doesn't work for a living or have some legal form of income**. If he is not independently wealthy, or have some other legal income, he will probably depend on you for support. Not only that, but **an**

idol mind is the devil's playground. That is asking for trouble.

Many women are perfectly willing to take care of a man, and allow him to be the stay at home, housemate, but men don't make good house-husbands when they don't have income and have to depend on someone else for support. Eventually, though not working, he'll be getting home just before you do, not having accomplished anything and will greet you (figuratively) with his hand out.

Encourage him to be somehow productive, though if it's not his will, it just becomes tougher on you. He needs to contribute to the relationship in as many ways as you do, or there will be no balance, and eventually you will resent him. Obviously whatever works for the relationship is most important, but don't forget about you.

Relationships go through **"the change of life"** just like individuals, and it will be vital that both parties remain in tune so that they can see what's happening and weather the storms. It's when the adjustments aren't made that the relationship becomes out of sync and in jeopardy.

Your man should live up to his potential, an that's and interpersonal issue that only he can deal with, but a little encouragement and tough love, can work wonders and never hurts. When working to reach his potential he'll learn that the limits are stretched and he is capable of doing more than he ever believed he could. Do not allow him to take the road less traveled just because it's easier or because it's more convenient. **"Beside Every Great Man is an even Greater Woman."** Be that great woman!

Men sometimes get spoiled and contribute less and less to the upkeep of the household, the cars, the kids, and even the relationship. Do not under any circumstances allow this to happen. Unless he is physically incapable, he should be no less busy around the house than you are. Doing chores around the house is not "helping you out," it's taking responsibility for his own domain. If you allow him to become lazy and unproductive, while wearing yourself out, then don't gripe and complain about what used to be.

A man has to be **"A MAN,"** in the relationship. Becoming **"A MAN"** is a process. Not every male is **"A MAN." "A MAN"** is responsible, caring protective, and goes the extra mile to make things better for those he cares about. He doesn't generally need the **"Honey Do" List.**

CHAPTER SEVEN

Relationships and Sports
Or
Sports and Relationships?

We've all heard that the way to a man's heart is through his stomach. Well, it ain't necessarily so. Women are without a doubt, number one on a man's list of life's priorities, however sports are right up there with women, sex and food.

Most boys grow up having been involved in some form of sports, whether it be playing, watching or listening. It was almost unmasculine, for a boy to reach the ripe old age of twelve and not have at least one favorite sport or idolize a major sports athlete.

Prior to appropriate recognition of gender equality in sports, fathers usually encourage the boys to join him in front of the tube, or accompany him to a baseball or football game, while "the girls" made cookies, in the kitchen with Mom. Little girls were given dolls at Christmas and the boys received baseball bats and gloves. Boys got athletic shoes and the girls got patton leathers. The boys got basketball jerseys and the girls got blouses with cute designs.

Sports hasn't just been something boys were introduced to. It's a part of who they became and started at an early age.

Many wives and life partners don't understand the fascination, with men tackling other men to keep from advancing with an oddly shaped ball, or hitting a little white golf ball hundreds of yards away only to retrieve it and repeat the process all over again. "Hard to understand," is an understatement!

Sports will always be a part of your man's life, no matter what. Few men don't have a sport that they're interested in. Most are fanatics about at least one and become very knowledgeable about the game and who's who in the sport.

Women who truly object to their man watching sports on televison at home, should consider changing their perspective. It should make you much more comfortable that he's watching it **at home.**

Women who have issues with their men so involved in such a ridiculous hobby should try to understand more about the sport and what makes him so drawn to it. Watch it on television with him, or go to a live game, having him explain the game, which he'll be glad to do. When you discover his level of knowledge and his excitement about it, maybe you'll want to know more. It's definitely one of the safest hobbies that a relationship can have and all guys have a healthier respect for women who are sports smart, or at least try.

Men are dedicated to sports and they're almost as excited about it as they are about sex. He'll race home from work, stay up late and sometimes even tune out that which he perceives irrelevant. When something good or bad happens, you'll have no problem understanding how he felt about it. When it's done and over, he's almost a different person, and nearly as exhausted as are the players.

Getting involved, is healthy advice. This is something a couple can do together and it doesn't necessarily cost anything that you're not already spending. It'll only strengthen your relationship.

CHAPTER EIGHT

Reignite the Passion in Your Relationship Make Sex and Intimacy a Part of Your Essence

Good relationships require lots of work. Relationships aren't just what happens to you, or what you do, it's your life and should be the best part of it.

All relationships have issues from time to time and the solution is all in the handling of the problems, disagreements and lulls, which they all have. Monotony leads to boredom and boredom leads to a thirst for something new and different.

All relationships have to be rejuvenated from time to time , because the tendency is to become comfortable with the way things are, and when you're comfortable, you don't usually want to change. *"Comfortable"* should not be the description of your relationship. This is the danger zone.

Nothing should become routine in your relationship. *"Routine"* is just another word for *"Boredom"* in a relationship. Nothing should be done just because that's the way you've always done it. It is no one else's job to make you happy. If you're not happy, don't keep it to yourself, and don't keep doing what makes you unhappy. Let him know how you feel and change what is getting in the way of your happiness. Don't place the burden totally on him, but make him a part of the action, make him aware and solicit his input, if the relationship is to continue.

Doing surprise nice-to-do things for each other when there's no special occasion, becomes more special than you know, and you'll be able to feel the power surge from your loving partner's acceptance and reaction.

Sex is a natural part of a romantic relationship. Every adult person has had some kind of sexual experience in his or her lifetime, even if they didn't realize what it was at the time. Abstinence in adulthood does not eliminate the urge. Sexual desire, and the way you feel about the person you're with, doesn't begin with sexual organs. It begins in the mind and/or the heart. More often than not, the initial physical affect or proof is arousal and eventual sex.

Sex is a vital component in a romantic relationship. *Intimacy* and expressions of love are what stabilizes the relationship and conveys meaning to each of the partners.

Sex is extremely powerful and pleasurable. Men are very visual and are often stimulated by the physical appearance of a woman. Men think of sex lots during the course of a day and to see a beautiful, sexy, well dressed woman, who appeals to his taste in women, definitely gets his attention.

All men and all women are attracted to members of the opposite gender, regardless of who's in their heart. It's normal and will never end. Acting on these feelings is what gets us into trouble and leads to cheating.

Everyday, when practicable, should involve some degree of intimacy, in the marriage or relationship.

Intimacy could be anything from a kiss and a hug, to sexual intercourse, and lots in between. Just "touching" can be sensual and therapeutic in a relationship.

The power of intimacy and sex is inestimable. Good, spontaneous, regular, passionate, sex is great and speaks volumes about the strength of your relationship.

Cheating for men is usually about sex, ego, conquest and even challenge. If he's a dog, he's going to be a dog anyway, and only he can change that, but doing your part, leaves no reason for feelings of guilt if you make a move.

CHAPTER NINE

Unconditional Love

Is there such an emotion as "Unconditional Love?" The closest we ever get to "unconditional love" is that of a **Mother's Love** for her child. No matter what the attitude, behavior, failures or bad decisions, generally speaking, a mother will always love her child.

Real love is an extremely powerful emotion and can withstand the worst kinds of bad weather.

Adversity in relationships, tests the limits and boundaries of love, and puts on display, the depth of commitment. A lack of love is clearly evident in bad times. In a loving marriage or a relationship, there is no hesitation to do the right thing.

Love between two people in a relationship or marriage can be seemably unbreakable, but unlike the love of a mother, it has its limits and boundaries. Sometimes the limits and boundaries are unclear, and can be stretched and changed, so it appears to be unconditional love, but in the long run, and after much negativity, it will fold.

Infidelity, is not acceptable in a relationship or marriage and should not be taken lightly. If your man strays and you decide to forgive him, then keep your word and forgive him. This is not to say that you will forget, but if he truly changes the unacceptable behavior, then you should honor your word, and give him space to do so. Rebuilding the trust, is terribly difficult, but if the relationship is to survive, behavioral adjustments must be made by both people. If you cannot forgive him, the relationship's last rites are waiting in queue.

CHAPTER TEN

His Actions Will Always Speak Louder Than His Words

It is common knowledge that men are easily distracted and have major difficulty keeping their eye on the prize, at times, the prize, being the relationship. Talk can be convincing, but actions are evidence, and irrefutable.

While words are important and sometimes impressive, and should be a valuable prelude for actions to follow, they are often without substance.

"Actions," are the bottom line, and are within the heart of the relationship. Watch what

a person does and you know who he is. If the words and the actions match, this is a true communication, and validates trust.

"I love you," means little coming from an abusive mate. "You are the only one," means little, if you know he cheats. "I'm sorry, I will never do it again," means nothing if you've heard it before, many times. Does he tell you how valuable you are, but forgets your birthday? Words have power and meaning, only when supported by the matching *"Action."*

About the Author

A middle-aged, first-time author, *MsterH*, is a student of human behavior and personal relationships.

He believes that the ladder of life is filled with both good and bad experiences, but that being truly in love with someone who can reciprocate that love in a similarly large way, makes the sometimes difficult climb up that ladder, much simpler to handle.

He believes that our history in relationships should make us smarter but should not control our future. That in life, we don't get unlimited opportunities to have what we truly want. That we are in control of our own happiness which takes on a more meaningful and precious character when shared with, "The One."

www.ingramcontent.com/pod-product-compliance
Lightning Source LLC
Chambersburg PA
CBHW061222280526
45784CB00006B/2588